T0083350

Exile Meditations

GABRIEL JACKSON

for SATB soloists or choir unaccompanied

MUSIC DEPARTMENT

OXFORD
UNIVERSITY PRESS

Commissioned by Christopher Walsh Sinka with the generous support of the Portland State University Department of Music (Ethan Sperry, Director of Choral Activities), the Latvian Relief Society of Canada (Daugavas Vanagi), and the following individual donors: Andris Bankovskis, Beth Ann Beck, Mārtiņš Bruveris, Lennie Cottrell, Ed Frazier Davis, Teresa Dragonetti, Paul French, Māris Graudiņš, Evan Hirsch, Bob Iofis, Linda Jakobsone, Bill Keaton, Egils Levits, Anna Marasco, Brendan Monte, Inese Nielsen, Alison Piasecka, Charlie Poe, Bart Pushaw, Gunta Reynolds, Andrejs Ritiņš, David Rothzeid, Susan Saunders, Solveiga Silkalna, Anna Sinka, Aivars and Nicola Sinka, Maija Sinka, Gilbert Spencer, Jeff and Denise Walsh, and Ģirts and Velga Zēgners.

First performed by Agnese Urka (soprano), Dārta Treija (alto), Christopher Walsh Sinka (tenor), and Eduards Fiskovičs (bass) at the Latvian Railway History Museum, Riga, on 30 July 2017.

Duration: 29 minutes

Soprano—also plays Brake Drum
Tenor—also plays Claves
Bass—also plays Railwayman's Whistle

If the piece is performed by SATB choir, then one singer from S, T, and B will also be required to play the minimal percussion parts.

TEXTS AND TRANSLATIONS

1.

Tās ilgas pēc dzimtenes brīvās,
Pēc zudušās mīļās un baltās,
Tās nevar izrunāt vārdos,
Tās nevar izdziedāt dziesmās,
Tās var vien izsāpēt, izsmelgt,
Tās klusi var izjust, var izciest
No stundas uz stundu lēnām,
No dienas uz dienu lēnām,
No gada uz gadu lēnām
Un līdzi ņemt kapā vai urnā.

That yearning for your free homeland,
Dear, precious and lost,
It cannot be put into words,
It cannot be turned into song,
It can only be lived through in pain,
It can only be quietly felt and endured
Hour after hour, slowly,
Day after day, slowly,
Year after year, slowly
And then taken with you to the urn or the grave.

Pēteris Ērmanis (1893–1969)
(English translation by Rita Ruduša)

2.

We journey towards a home not of our flesh. Its chestnut trees are not of our bones.
Its rocks are not like goats in the mountain hymn. The pebbles' eyes are not lilies.
We journey towards a home that does not halo our heads with a special sun.
Mythical women applaud us. A sea for us, a sea against us.
When water and wheat are not at hand, eat our love and drink our tears...
There are mourning scarves for poets. A row of marble statues will lift our voice.
And an urn to keep the dust of time away from our souls. Roses for us and against us.
You have your glory, we have ours. Of our home we see only the unseen: our mystery.
Glory is ours: a throne carried on feet torn by roads that led to every home but our own!
The soul must recognize itself in its very soul, or die here.

Mahmoud Darwish (1941–2008)

3.

Nav sava kapa,
nav sava krusta.
Nav pat sava vārda...
It kā tu nebūtu
dzimis, ne miris.
Tik ūpji mēdās,
maitu putni kraukļi
biezokņos tumšos.
Gaudo tik vilki
puteņu naktīs.
Kāpj kāvi debesīs
liesmainos mēteļos.
Meklē tavu kapu,
meklē tavu vārdu.
Nevar atrast.

No grave of your own,
No cross of your own.
Not even a name...
As if you had neither
been born nor died.
Only owls cry mockingly,
Ravens, scavenger birds
In the dark woods.
Only wolves howl
In winter blizzard.
Northern lights rise skyward
In their fiery cloaks,
Searching for your grave,
Searching for your name.
Not finding one.

Rūta Skujiņa (1907–64)
(English translation by Rita Ruduša)

4.

The night became long and the dark increased,
but I didn't find starlight to indicate the path.
The trip became long, and my footsteps began
to disappear, without them how would I find a way back...
I doze off with a dream petting my eyeball.
At the same time I fear the daybreak will bury me.
Don't ask about me.
Don't ask who I am.

Ammar Tabbab (b. 1984)

5.

Ir miljons mūs, ko pazīst daudzi,
Kā kailus burtus – D un P.
Mūs iztrenca kā bišu draudzi,
Kad stropu dūmiem izsvēpē.
    Mums nav vairs cerības nevienas,
    Tik pārtiekam no vakardienas.

Tur ungārs ugunīgs no Pustas,
Tur polis mieru neatrod.
Te latvietis kā ēna kustas,
Lūdz Dievam: manu zemi dod!
    Nav gan vairs cerības nevienas,
    Mums jāpārtiek no vakardienas.

Skumst brālis lietuvis no Kaunas,
Met čukstot krustu ukrainis.
Lai atkal noautos, drūms aunas
Ik rītu mājup igaunis.
    Bet nav vairs cerības nevienas,
    Tik jāpārtiek no vakardienas.

No gada gadā rieciens plānāks,
Bet augumā aug izsalkums.
Jau gaidām sen, kad, "lielie" sanāks
Un nolaupīto atdos mums.
    Āi, nav vairs cerības nevienas,
    Lemts pārtikt mums no vakardienas.

A million there, albeit for many, we go
By simply D and P.
Akin to family made homeless,
Smoked out from our hive of bees.
    We have no ray of hope today,
    And living off our yesterday.

A hot Hungarian is here from Puszta,
A Pole who finds no peace.
A Latvian walks shadow-like, praying,
Give me my land back, please!
    We truly have no hope today,
    And have to live off yesterday.

A Lithuanian, from Kaunas, forlorn,
A Ukrainian, whispering, crosses his heart.
An Estonian is homeward bound each morning,
Only to take his shoes off, every night.
    But we have no hope left today,
    And only live off yesterday.

From year to year the slice gets thinner,
While our hunger swells and grows.
For long we've waited: "Big Ones", gather
And give us back our stolen shores.
    Oh, not a ray of hope today,
    We're meant to live off yesterday.

Teodors Zeltiņš (1914–91)
(English translation by Rita Ruduša)

6.

Earth is pressing against us, trapping us in the final passage.
To pass through, we pull off our limbs.
Earth is squeezing us. If only we were its wheat, we might die and yet live.
If only it were our mother so that she might temper us with mercy.
If only we were pictures of rocks held in our dreams like mirrors.
We glimpse faces in their final battle for the soul, of those who will be killed
by the last living among us. We mourn their children's feast.
We saw the faces of those who would throw our children out of the windows
of this last space. A star to burnish our mirrors.
Where should we go after the last border? Where should birds fly after the last sky?
Where should plants sleep after the last breath of air?
We write our names with crimson mist!
We end the hymn with our flesh.
Here we will die. Here, in the final passage.
Here or there, our blood will plant olive trees.

Mahmoud Darwish (1941–2008)

7.

Tur, savā zemē, bij man sava sēta,
To atstāju es bargā likteņvarā,
Kaut mani dēli gāja par to karā—
    Tā audžu audzēm bija svēta.

Tik vien es līdzi aiznesu no mājas
Kā sauju zemes. Kaisiet to pār šķirstu
Man kapā, kad es svešā zemē mirstu—
    Lai tā pār maniem pīšļiem klājas.

There, in my homeland, I had a homestead.
I left it in the hands of cruel fate,
Even if my sons had gone to war for it—
    Even if, for generations, it had been sacred.

All I had brought with me from home
Is a handful of soil. Scatter it over my coffin,
In the grave in a foreign land when I die—
    Let it cover my remains.

Kārlis Dziļleja (1891–1963)
(English translation by Rita Ruduša)

LATVIAN PRONUNCIATION GUIDE

ā = long 'a' as in h**a**rd
ē = long 'a' as in m**a**de
ī = 'ee' as in s**ee**
o = 'oer' as in d**oer**
u = 'oo' as in f**oo**t

c = 'ts' as in ha**ts**
č = 'ch' as in **ch**ess
g = hard 'g' as in **g**arment
j = 'y' as in **y**ellow
k = hard 'c' as in **c**ard
ķ = 'ty' as in Ka**ty**a
ļ = 'll' as in mi**ll**ion

ū = 'oo' as in f**oo**d
ie = 'ie' as in happ**ie**r
ai = 'i' as in m**i**ne
au = 'ow' as in c**ow**

ņ = 'ny' as in ca**ny**on
r = rolled 'r'
s = 'c' as in **c**ity
š = 'sh' as in **sh**ip
z = 'z' as in **z**ebra
ž = 's' as in mea**s**ure

Where a note has a duration of a crotchet or more, the first vowel of a diphthong should last one quaver, regardless of the total length of the note; where less than a crotchet, the first vowel should last one semiquaver.

for those in exile, past and present

Exile Meditations

GABRIEL JACKSON

1.

Pēteris Ērmanis (1893–1969)

Music © Oxford University Press 2019.
Texts by Skujiņa, Zeltiņš, and Dziļleja licensed courtesy of AKKA/LAA;
Darwish texts © 2013 by the Regents of the University of California. Published by the University of California Press;
Tabbab text © Ammar Tabbab. Used by permission.

Duration: 29 mins

Printed in Great Britain

OXFORD UNIVERSITY PRESS, MUSIC DEPARTMENT, GREAT CLARENDON STREET, OXFORD OX2 6DP
The Moral Rights of the Composer have been asserted. Photocopying this copyright material is ILLEGAL.

13
mp mf f mp
Pēc zu-du - šās, pēc zu-du - šās mī - ļās, pēc zu-du - šās mi - ļās un bal - tās,
Pēc zu-du - šās, pēc zu-du - šās mī - ļās, pēc zu-du - šās mi - ļās un bal - tās,
Pēc zu-du - šās, pēc zu-du - šās mī - ļās, pēc zu-du - šās mi - ļās un bal - tās,
Pēc zu-du - šās, pēc zu-du - šās mī - ļās, pēc zu-du - šās mi - ļās un bal - tās,

21
mf p
pēc zu - du - šās mī - ļās un bal - - tās,
pēc zu - du - - šās mī - ļās un bal - tās,
p mf
pēc zu - du - šās mī - ļās un bal - - - tās, Tās ne -
mf
Tās ne -

28
mf p
vār - - - - dos,
mf p
vār - - - dos,
mf
-var iz - ru - nāt, Tās ne - var iz -
mf
- var iz - ru - nāt, Tās ne - var

36
mf
p
mf
dzies - - - - mās, iz - -
dzies - - - - mās, iz - -
- dzie - dāt dzies - - mās, Tās var vien iz - -
iz - dzie - dāt, Tās var vien iz -
44
mp
mf
-sā - pēt, iz - smelgt, Tās klu - si var iz - just, var iz -
-sā - pēt, iz - smelgt, Tās klu - si var iz - just, var
-sā - pēt, iz - smelgt, Tās klu - si var iz - just, var iz -
-sā - pēt, iz - smelgt,
51
p
- ciest lē - nām,
iz - ciest No stun - das uz stun - du, No
- ciest No stun - das uz stun - du, No

62
p
lē - nām,
die - nas uz die - nu,
No ga - da uz ga - du,
die - nas uz die - nu,
No ga - da uz ga - du,

74
p
f
mf
lē - - - nām
Un lī - dzi ņemt ka - pā vai ur - nā,
Un lī - dzi ņemt ka-pā vai ur-nā,
Un lī - dzi ņemt ka - pā vai ur - nā,
Un lī - dzi ņemt ka-pā vai ur-nā,

83
mp
p
ka-pā vai ur-nā.
ka-pā vai ur-nā.
ka-pā vai ur-nā.
un lī - dzi ņemt ka - pā vai ur - nā.

2.

Mahmoud Darwish (1941–2008)

Quite quick ♩ = *c.*84

16
p
mf
- lies. We jour - ney to - wards a
- lies. We jour - ney to - wards a
not li - lies. We jour - ney to - wards a
not li - lies. We jour - ney to - wards a
22
p
mf
mp
home that does not ha - lo our heads with a spe-cial sun.
home that does not ha - lo our heads with a spe-cial sun.
home that does not ha - lo our heads with a spe-cial sun.
home that does not ha - lo our heads with a spe - cial sun.
28
mp
p
3
Myth - - ic - al wo-men ap - plaud us.
Myth - ic-al wo - men ap - plaud us.
Myth - - ic - al wo-men ap - plaud us.
Myth - ic - al wo - men ap - plaud us.

33
f
p
mp
A sea for us, a sea a - gainst us. When
39
mf
mp
wa - - - - - - ter and wheat are not at
44
hand, eat our love and drink our tears...

52
p
There are mourn - - ing scarves for po - - ets. A
There are mourn - ing scarves for po - ets. A
There are mourn - - ing scarves for po - - ets. A
There are mourn - ing scarves for po - ets. A
59
row of mar - ble sta - tues will lift our
row of mar - - ble sta - - tues will lift our
row of mar - ble sta - tues will lift our
row of mar - - ble sta - - tues will lift our
65
mf
mp
voice. And an urn to keep the dust
voice. And an urn to keep the dust
voice. And an urn to keep the dust
voice. And an urn to keep the dust

72
p
of time a - way from our souls.
of time a - way from our souls.
of time a - way from our souls.
of time a - way from our souls.
78
f
p
mf
Ro - ses for us and a - gainst us. You have
Ro - ses for us and a - gainst us. You have
Ro - ses for us and a - gainst us. You have
Ro - ses for us and a - gainst us. You have
84
f
p
your glo - - - - - - ry, we have ours.
your glo - - - - - - ry, we have ours.
your glo - - - - - - ry, we have ours.
your glo - - - - - - ry, we have ours.

91
mf
f
Of our home we see on-ly the un - seen:
Of our home we see on - ly the un - seen:
Of our home we see on - ly the un - seen:
Of our home we see on - ly the un - seen:
97
pp
ff
our my - ste - ry. Glo - - - - - -
our my - ste - ry. Glo - - - - - -
our my - ste - ry. Glo - - - - - -
our my - ste - ry. Glo - - - - - -
103
-ry is ours: a throne car -
- ry is ours: a throne car -
-ry is ours: a throne car -
- ry is ours: a throne car -

108
- ried on feet torn from roads that led to
-ried on feet torn from roads that led to
- ried on feet torn from roads that led
-ried on feet torn from roads that led
113
ev - 'ry home but our own! The soul must re-cog - nize it -
ev - 'ry home but our own! The soul must re-cog - nize it -
to ev - 'ry home but our own! The soul must re-cog - nize it -
to ev - 'ry home but our own! The soul must re-cog - nize it -
p
121
-self in its ve - ry soul, or die here.
-self in its ve - ry soul, or die here.
-self in its ve - ry soul, or die here.
-self in its ve - ry soul, or die here.
pp

3.

Rūta Skujiņa (1907–64)

19
mp
p
ne-bū - tu dzi - mis, ne mi - - - - - ris.
ne-bū - tu dzi - mis, ne mi - ris, mi - ris.
ne-bū - tu dzi - mis, ne mi - - - - - ris.
ne-bū - tu dzi - mis, ne mi - ris, mi - ris.
25
f
3
Tik ū - ū - ū - ū - ū - pji mē-ē - ē-dās,
Tik ū - ū - ū - ū - ū - pji mē-ē - ē-dās,
Tik ū - ū - ū - ū - ū - pji mē-ē - ē-dās,
Tik ū - ū - ū - ū - ū - pji mē-ē - ē-dās,
29
mai - tu, mai - tu pu-u - u - u-u - u - u - u - tni krau-au-au-kļi bie - -
mai - tu, mai - tu pu-u - u - u-u - u - u - u - tni krau-au-au-kļi bie - -
mai - tu, mai - tu pu-u - u - u-u - u - u - u - tni krau-au-au-kļi bie - -
mai - tu, mai - tu pu-u - u - u-u - u - u - u - tni krau-au-au-kļi bie - -

33
ff
-zok - ņos tum - šos.
Gau - do tik vi - lki pu - te - ņu
p
37
na - - - ktīs.
Kāpj
42
kā - vi de-e-e-e-e-e-e - be - sīs lie - smai - nos mē-te - ļos.

49
Me - klē ta - vu ka - - - - - - - pu,
Me-klē ta-vu ka-pu,
Me-klē ta-vu ka-pu,
Me-klē ta-vu ka-pu,
54
f
me - klē ta - vu vār - - - - - - - du.
me-klē ta-vu vār-du,
me-klē ta-vu vār-du,
me-klē ta-vu vār-du,
59
mf
mp
me - klē ta - vu vār - du, vār - du,
me-klē ta-vu vār-du, vār-du,
me-klē ta-vu vār-du, vār-du,
me-klē ta-vu vār-du, vār-du,

65
p
vār - - - - - - - - du.
pp
Ne-var
vār-du.
Ne-var
Claves
vār-du.
Ne-var
vār-du.
Ne-var
71
a - trast.
a - trast.
a - trast.
a - trast, a - - - - trast,
77
a - - trast, a - - trast.

4.

Ammar Tabbab (b. 1984)

Very slow ♩ = *c.* 52

ff

The night, the night be-came, the night be-came, be-came, the night be-came long,

ff

The night, the night be-came, the night be-came, be-came, the night be-came long,

ff

The night, the night be-came, the night be-came, be-came, the night be-came long,

ff

The night, the night be-came, the night be-came, be-came, the night be-came long,

8

pp

the night be-came long and the dark in - creased, but I did-n't find star-light to in - di -

pp

the night be-came long and the dark in - creased, but I did-n't find star-light to in - di -

pp

the night be-came long and the dark in - creased, but I did-n't find star-light to in - di -

pp

the night be-came long and the dark in - creased, but I did-n't find star-light to in - di -

17

-cate the path. The trip be-came long, and my foot-steps be - gan to dis-ap - pear, with-

-cate the path. The trip be-came long, and my foot-steps be - gan to dis-ap - pear, with-

-cate the path. The trip be-came long, and my foot-steps be - gan to dis-ap - pear, with-

-cate the path. The trip be-came long, and my foot-steps be - gan to dis-ap - pear, with-

26
-out them how would I find a way back... I doze off with a dream
-out them how would I find a way back... I doze off with a dream
-out them how would I find a way back... I doze off with a dream
-out them how would I find a way back... I doze off with a dream
36
pet-ting my eye-ball. At the same time I fear the day - break will
pet-ting my eye-ball. At the same time I fear the day - break will
pet-ting my eye-ball. At the same time I fear the day - break will
pet-ting my eye-ball. At the same time I fear the day - break will
44
f
p
bu-ry me. Don't ask a-bout me. Don't ask who I am.
bu-ry me. Don't ask a-bout me. Don't ask who I am.
bu-ry me. Don't ask a-bout me. Don't ask who I am.
bu-ry me. Don't ask a-bout me. Don't ask who I am.

5.

Teodors Zeltiņš (1914–91)

24
p
mf
mp
izs - vē - pē. Mums nav vairs ce - rī - bas ne - vie
izs - vē - pē. Mums nav vairs ce - rī - bas,
- pu, izs - vē - pē. Mums nav vairs ce - rī - bas,
izs- -pē. Mums nav vairs ce - rī - bas,
32
p
- nas,
Tik pār - tie - kam no va - kar - die - nas.
41
mp
mf
Tur un - gārs u - gu - nīgs no Pu - - stas, Tur po -
Tur un - gārs u - gu - nīgs no Pu - - stas, Tur po -
Tur un - gārs u - gu - nīgs no Pu -

49
mf
mp
-lis mie - - ru ne - a - - - trod. Te
-lis mie - - ru ne - a - - - trod. Te
- stas, u - gu - nīgs no Pu - stas. Te
Pu - - stas. Te
56
mf
mp
mf
lat - vie - tis kā ē - na ku - stas, Lūdz Die - vam: ma - nu
lat - - vie - - tis kā... Lūdz Die - vam: ma - nu
p
lat - - vie - - tis kā... Die - - vam,
lat - vie - tis kā ē - na ku - stas, Die - - vam,
64
mp
mf
ze - mi dod! Nav gan vairs ce - rī - - bas
ze - mi dod! Nav gan vairs ce - rī - bas,
lūdz, lūdz Die - vam... Nav gan vairs ce - rī - bas,
Die - - vam... Nav gan vairs ce - rī - bas,

71
mp
p
ne - vie - nas,
Mums jā - pār - tiek no va - kar -
Mums jā - pār - tiek no va - kar -
Mums jā - pār - tiek no va - kar -
79
mp
-die - nas. Skumst brā - lis lie - - tu -
-die - nas. Skumst brā - lis lie - tu - vis no
mf
-die - nas. Skumst brā - lis lie - tu - vis no
85
- - vis no Kau - - nas, lie - - tu -
Kau - - - nas, Met čuk - stot kru - - -
Kau - - - nas, Met čuk - stot kru - - -

91
mp
mf
Kau - - nas, Lai at - kal no -
- vis no Kau - nas, Lai at - - kal
mp
-tu u - krai - - - nis. Lai at - - kal
mp
mf
-tu u - krai - - - nis. Lai at - kal no -
98
mp
p
-au - tos, drūms au - nas rī - - tu, rī -
p
no - au... rī - - tu, ik, ik
mf
no - au... Ik rī - tu mā - jup i -
mp
mf
-au - tos, drūms au - nas Ik rī - tu mā - jup i -
105
mf
mp
- - tu... Bet nav vairs ce - rī - - bas ne - vie-
mf
mp
rī - tu... Bet nav vairs ce - rī - bas,
mp
mf
mp
-gau - nis. Bet nav vairs ce - rī - bas,
mp
mf
mp
-gau - nis. Bet nav vairs ce - rī - bas,

112
p
- nas,
Tik jā - pār - tiek no va - kar - die - nas.
Tik jā - pār - tiek no va - kar - die - nas.
Tik jā - pār - tiek no va - kar - die - nas.
120
f
No ga - da ga - dā rie - ciens plā - nāks,
No ga - da ga - dā rie - ciens plā - nāks,
No ga - da ga - dā rie - ciens plā - nāks,
No ga - da ga - dā rie - ciens plā - nāks,
128
pp
mp
Bet au - gu - mā aug iz - sal - kums. Jau gai -
Bet au - gu - mā aug iz - sal - kums. Jau gai -
Bet au - gu - mā aug iz - sal - kums. Jau gai - dām
Bet au - gu - mā aug iz - sal - kums. Jau gai - dām

137
p
-dām, jau gai - dām sen, Un no - lau - pī - to at -
p
-dām, jau gai - dām sen, Un no - lau - pī - to at -
mf
mp
p
sen, kad, "lie - lie" sa - nāks Un no - lau - pī - to at -
mf
mp
p
sen, kad, "lie - lie" sa - nāks Un no - lau - pī - to at -
145
ff
f
-dos mums. Āi, nav vairs ce - rī - bas ne - vie -
ff
f
-dos mums. Āi, nav vairs ce - rī - bas,
ff
f
-dos mums. Āi, nav vairs ce - rī - bas,
ff
f
-dos mums. Āi, nav vairs ce - rī - bas,
152
mf
p
- nas, ne - vie - nas.
p
Lemts pār-tikt mums no va-kar - die - nas.
p
Lemts pār-tikt mums no va-kar - die - nas.
p
Lemts pār-tikt mums no va-kar - die - nas.

6.

Mahmoud Darwish

22
earth is, earth is, squeez-ing, squeez-ing, earth is squeez-ing, squeez-ing, squeez-ing, earth, earth is squeez-ing,
earth is, earth is, squeez-ing, squeez-ing, earth is squeez-ing, squeez-ing, squeez-ing, earth, earth is squeez-ing,
earth is, earth is, squeez-ing, squeez-ing, earth is squeez-ing, squeez-ing, squeez-ing, earth, earth is squeez-ing,

29
If on - ly we were
earth is squeez-ing, earth is, earth is squeez-ing, squee - zing us. If on - ly we
earth is squeez-ing, earth is, earth is squeez-ing, squee - zing us.
earth is squeez-ing, earth is, earth is squeez-ing, squee - zing us.

36
its wheat, we might die and yet live.
were its wheat, we might die and yet live.
If on - ly it
If on - ly

43
were our mo-ther so that she might tem - per us with
it were our mo-ther so that she might tem - per us with
51
f
If on - ly we were pic-tures of rocks held in our
If on - ly we were pic-tures of rocks held in our
mer - cy. If on - ly we were pic-tures of rocks held in our
mer - cy. If on - ly we were pic-tures of rocks held in our
58
pp
dreams like mir - rors. We glimpse fa-ces in their fi-nal bat-tle
dreams like mir - rors. We glimpse fa-ces in their fi-nal bat-tle
dreams like mir - rors. We glimpse fa-ces in their fi-nal bat-tle
dreams like mir - rors.

65
for the soul, of those who will be killed by the last liv-ing a - mong us.
for the soul, of those who will be killed by the last liv-ing a - mong us.
for the soul, of those who will be killed by the last liv-ing a - mong us.

73
mf
pp
We mourn their child - ren's feast. We saw the fa-ces of those who would throw our
We mourn their child - ren's feast. We saw the fa-ces of those who would throw our
We mourn their child - ren's feast. We saw the fa-ces of those who would throw our
We mourn their child - ren's feast.

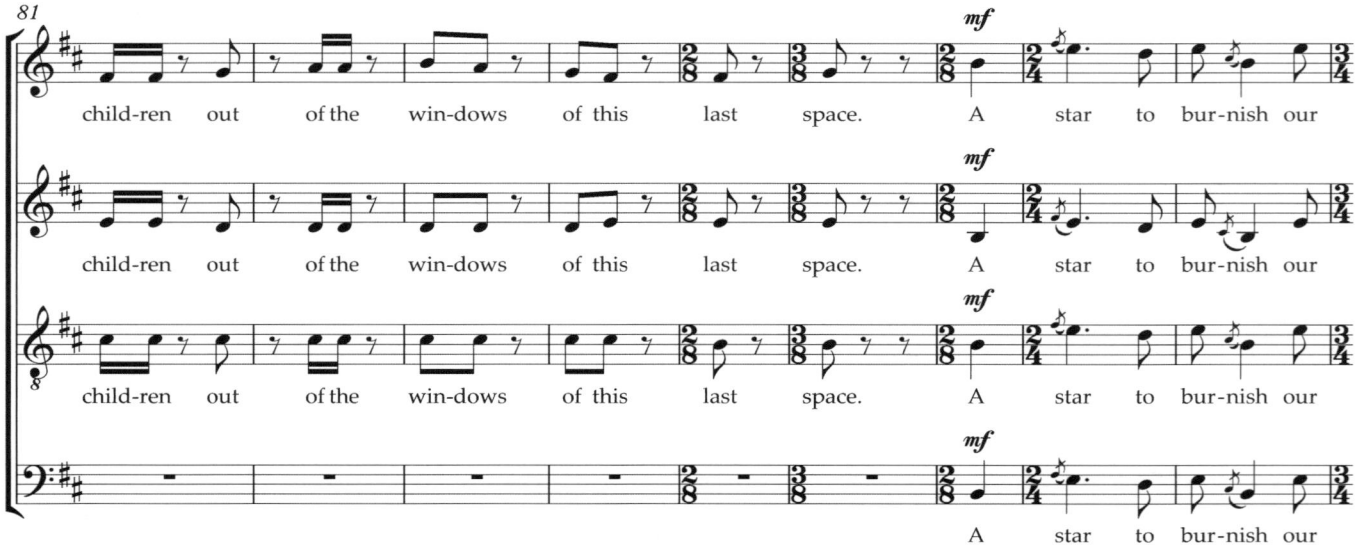
81
mf
child-ren out of the win-dows of this last space. A star to bur-nish our
child-ren out of the win-dows of this last space. A star to bur-nish our
child-ren out of the win-dows of this last space. A star to bur-nish our
A star to bur-nish our

90
p
mir-rors. Where should we go af - ter the last bor-der?
mir-rors. Where should we go af-ter the last bor - der?
mir-rors. Where should we...?
mir-rors. Where should we...?
96
mp
Where should birds fly af - ter the last sky?
Where should birds fly af-ter the last sky?
Where should birds...?
Where should birds...?
101
mf
p
Where should plants sleep af - ter the last breath of air? We
Where should plants sleep af - ter the last breath of air? We
Where should plants...? We
Where should plants...? We

107
mf
mp
write our names with cri - i - i - i - i - im - son mist! We end the
113
f
p
ff
hymn with our fle - e - e - e - e - e - e - esh. Here we, here we will, we will,
120
here we, we will, here we will, here we will, here we will, we will,

Brake drum
hit with hammer
126
ff
pp
here we will die. Here we will die. Here, in the fi - nal
here we will die. Here we will die. Here, in the fi - nal
here we will die. Here we will die. Here, in the fi - nal
here we will die. Here we will die. Here, in the fi - nal
133
p
mf
p
pas - sage. Here or there, our blood will plant
pas - sage. Here or there, our blood will plant
pas - sage. Here or there, our blood will plant
pas - sage. Here or there, our blood will plant
138
mp
mf
mp
o - - - - - - - live trees.
o - - - - - - - live trees.
o - - - - - - - live trees.
o - - - - - - - - live trees.

7.

Kārlis Dziļleja (1891–1963)

Slow ♩ = *c.* 60

p *mp* *p*

Tur, sa - vā ze - mē, bij man sa - va sē - ta,

Tur, sa - vā ze - mē, bij man sa - va sē - ta,

Tur, sa - vā ze - mē, bij man sa - va sē - ta,

Tur, sa - vā ze - mē, bij man sa - va sē - ta,

8

mp *mf* *mp* *mf*

To at - stā - ju es bar - gā lik - teń - va - rā, Kaut ma - ni

To at - stā - ju es bar - gā lik - teń - va - rā, Kaut ma - ni

To at - stā - ju es bar - gā lik - teń - va - rā, Kaut ma - ni

To at - stā - ju es bar - gā lik - teń - va - rā, Kaut ma - ni

15

mp *p*

dē - li gā - ja par to ka - rā— Tā aud - žu

dē - li gā - ja par to ka - rā— Tā aud - žu

dē - li gā - ja par to ka - rā— Tā aud - žu

dē - li gā - ja par to ka - rā— Tā aud - žu

22
mp
p
mf
aud - zēm bi - - - ja svē - ta. Tik
aud - zēm bi - - - ja svē - ta. Tik
aud - zēm bi - - - ja svē - ta. Tik
aud - zēm bi - - - ja svē - ta. Tik
29
f
vien es lī - dzi aiz - ne - su no mā - jas Kā sau - ju
vien es lī - dzi aiz - ne - su no mā - jas Kā sau - ju
vien es lī - dzi aiz - ne - su no mā - jas Kā sau - ju
vien es lī - dzi aiz - ne - su no mā - jas Kā sau - ju
36
mp
mf
f
mf
ze - mes. Kai - siet to pār škir - stu Man ka - pā,
ze - mes. Kai - siet to pār škir - stu Man ka - pā,
ze - mes. Kai - siet to pār škir - stu Man ka - pā,
ze - mes. Kai - siet to pār škir - stu Man ka - pā,

Brockley/Bloomsbury/Guildford, March–June 2017